Girls, girls, girls

Adult coloring book

La Fresa

Copyright©2017 La Fresa
All Rights Reserved

Copyright © 2017 by La Fresa

All rights reserved. No part of this publication may be reproduced, distributed, or transmitted in any form or by any means, including photocopying, recording, or other electronic or mechanical methods, without the prior written permission of the author, except in the case of brief quotations embodied in critical reviews and certain other noncommercial uses permitted by copyright law.

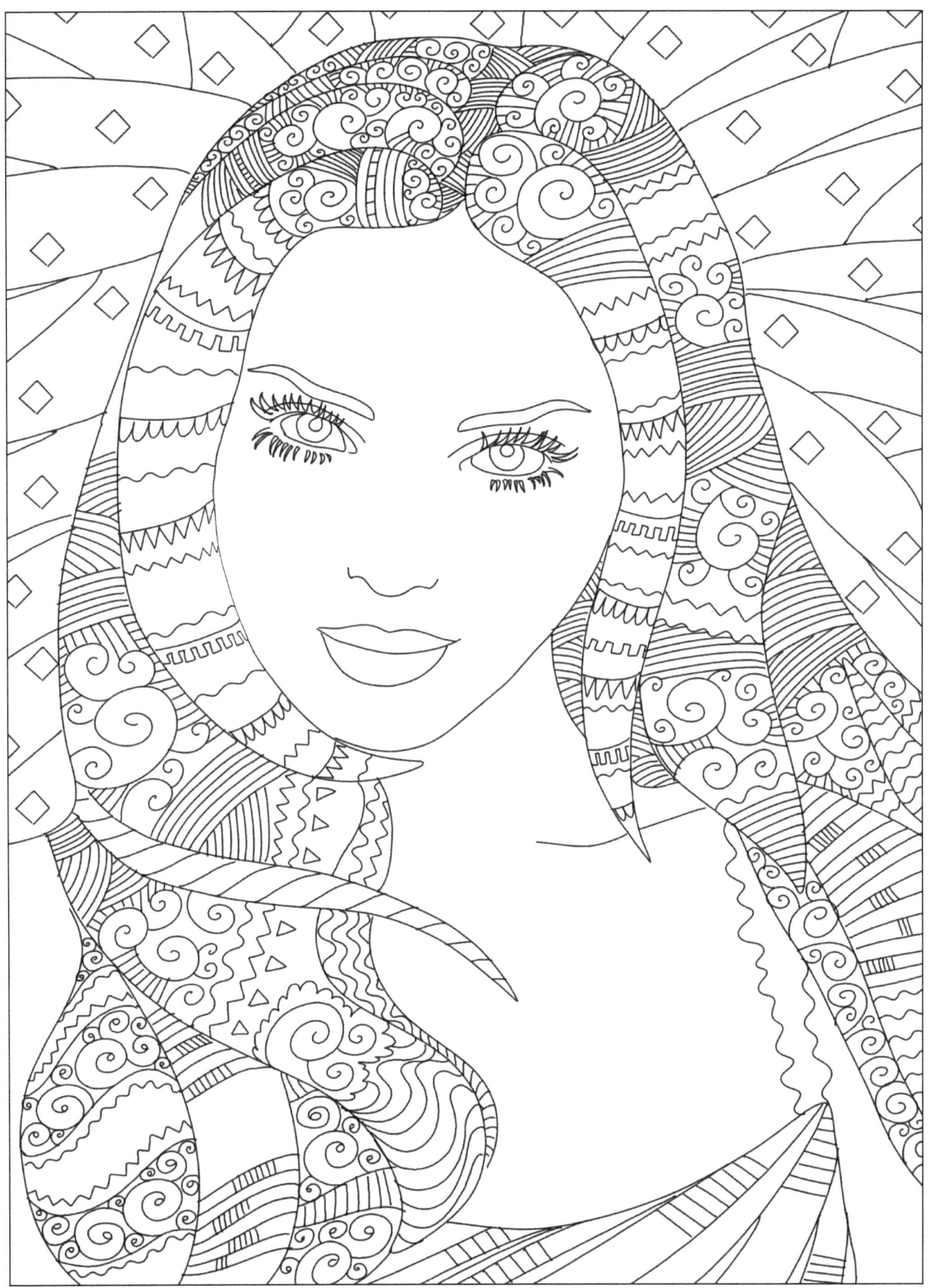

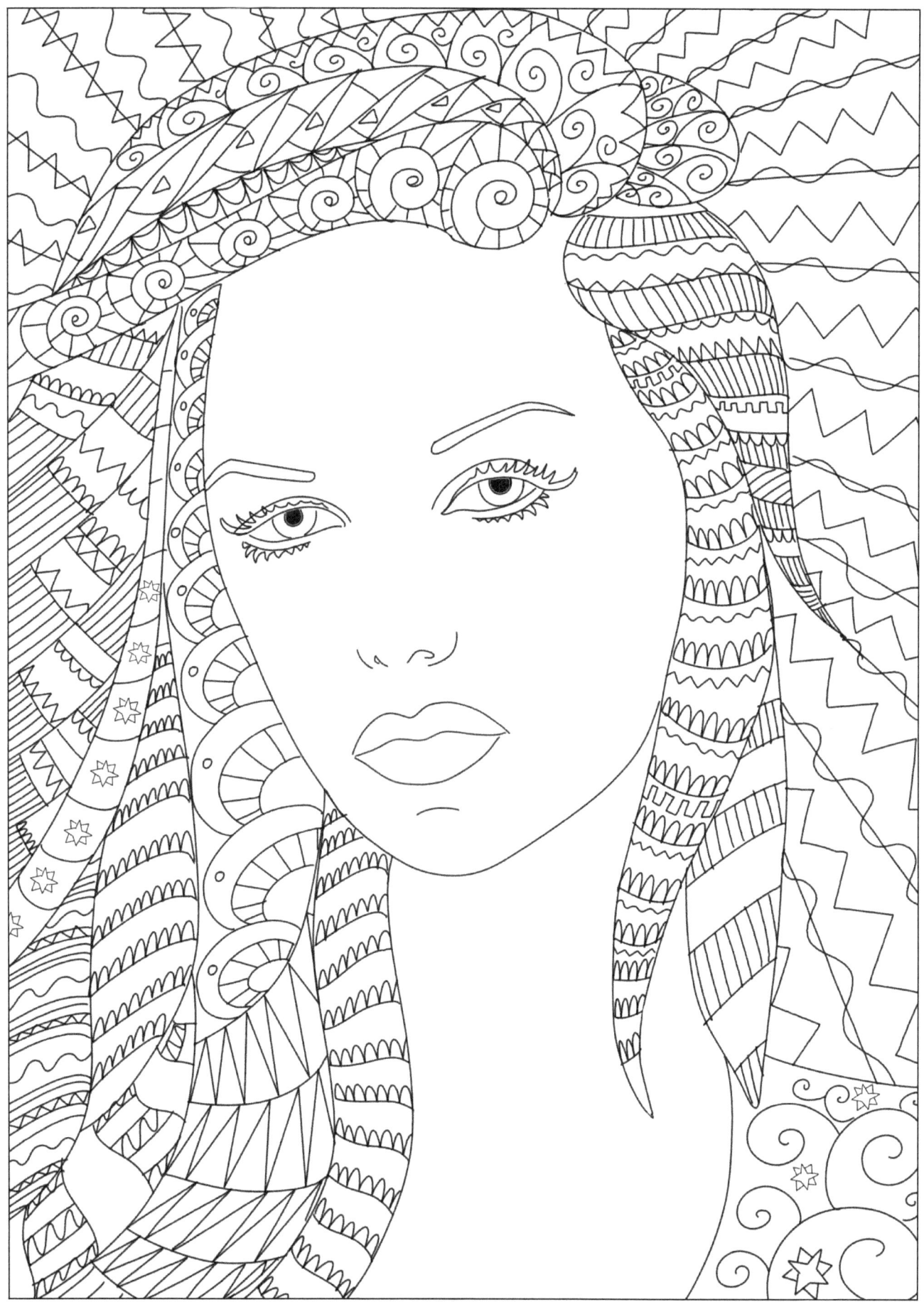

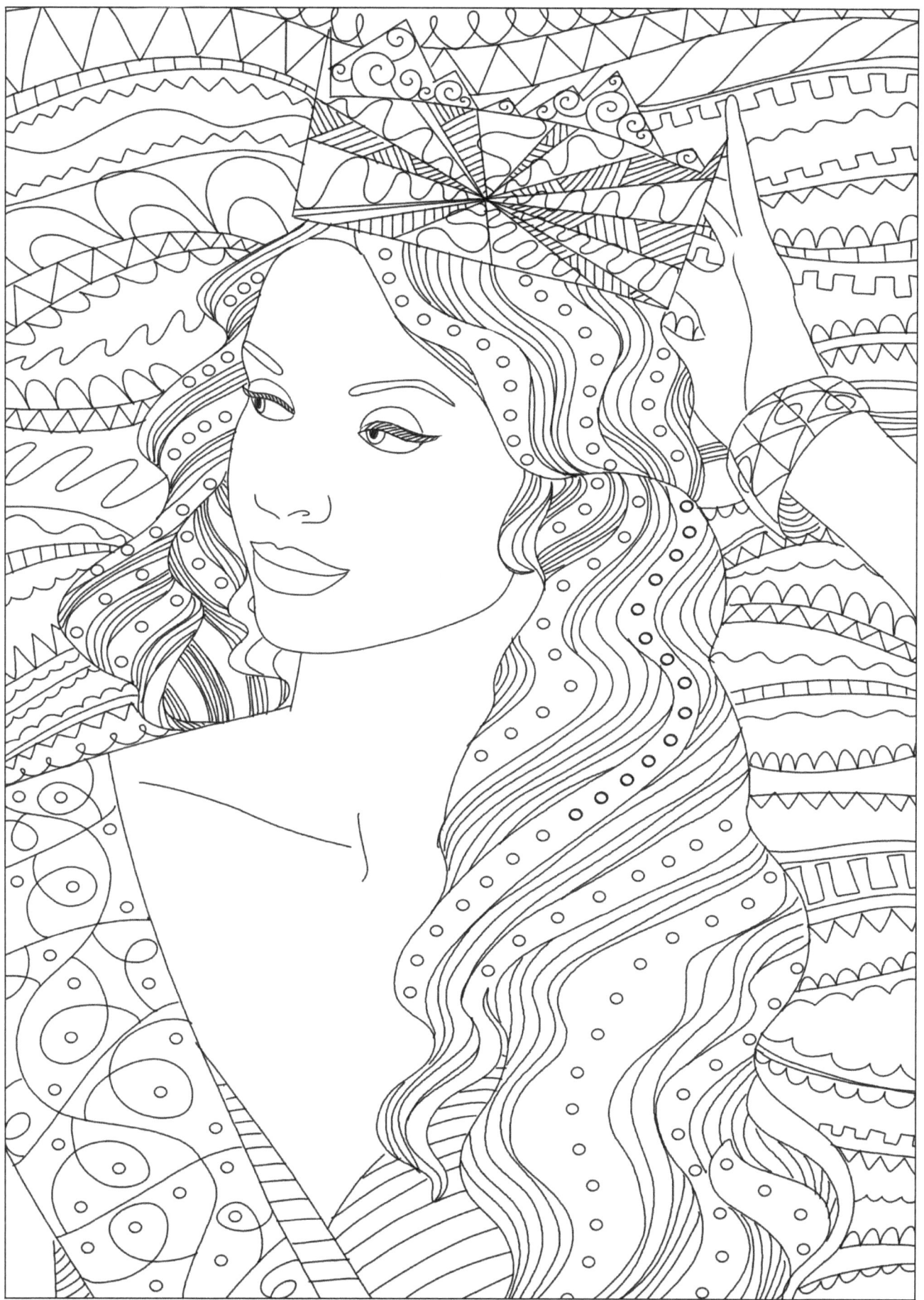

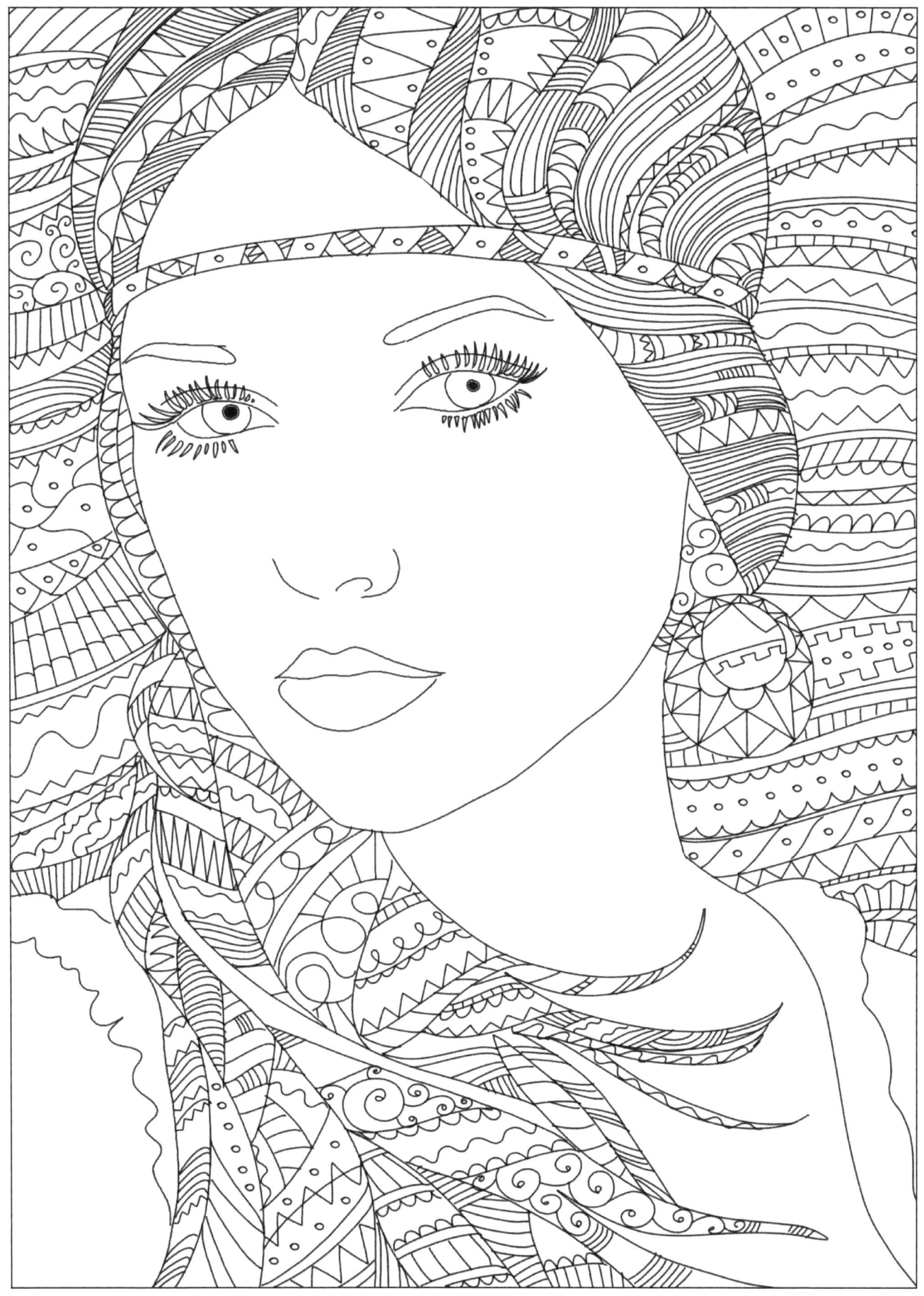

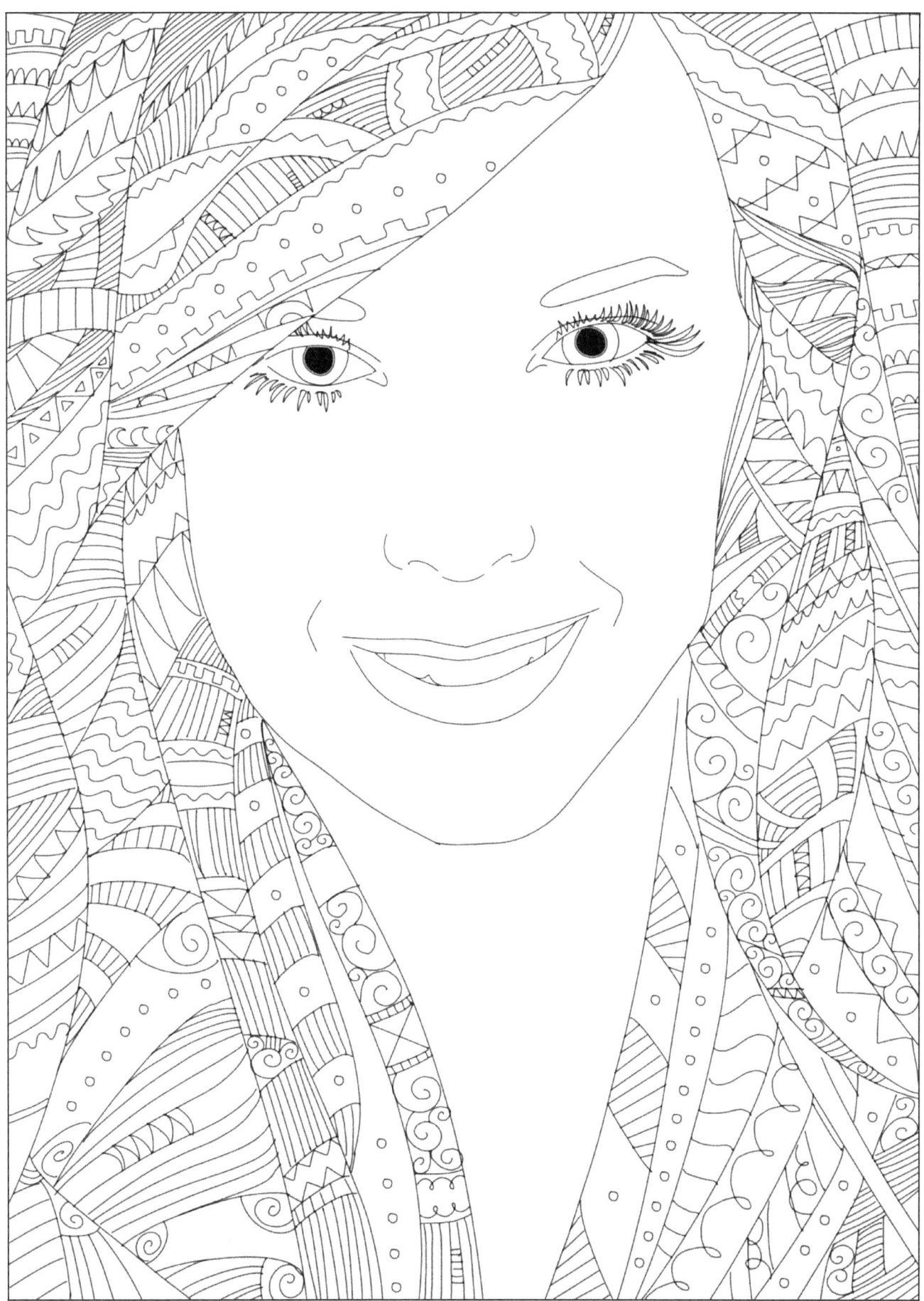

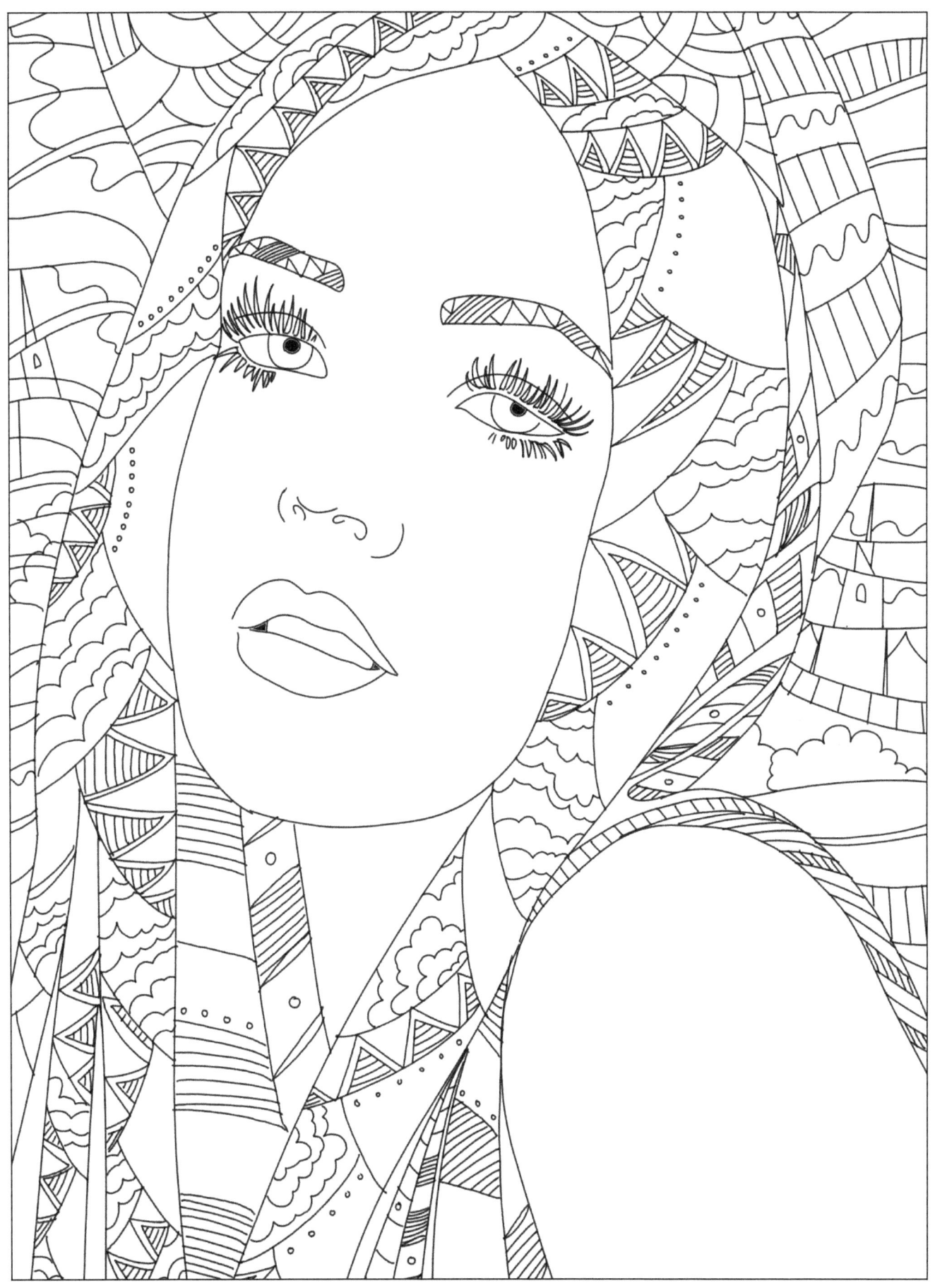

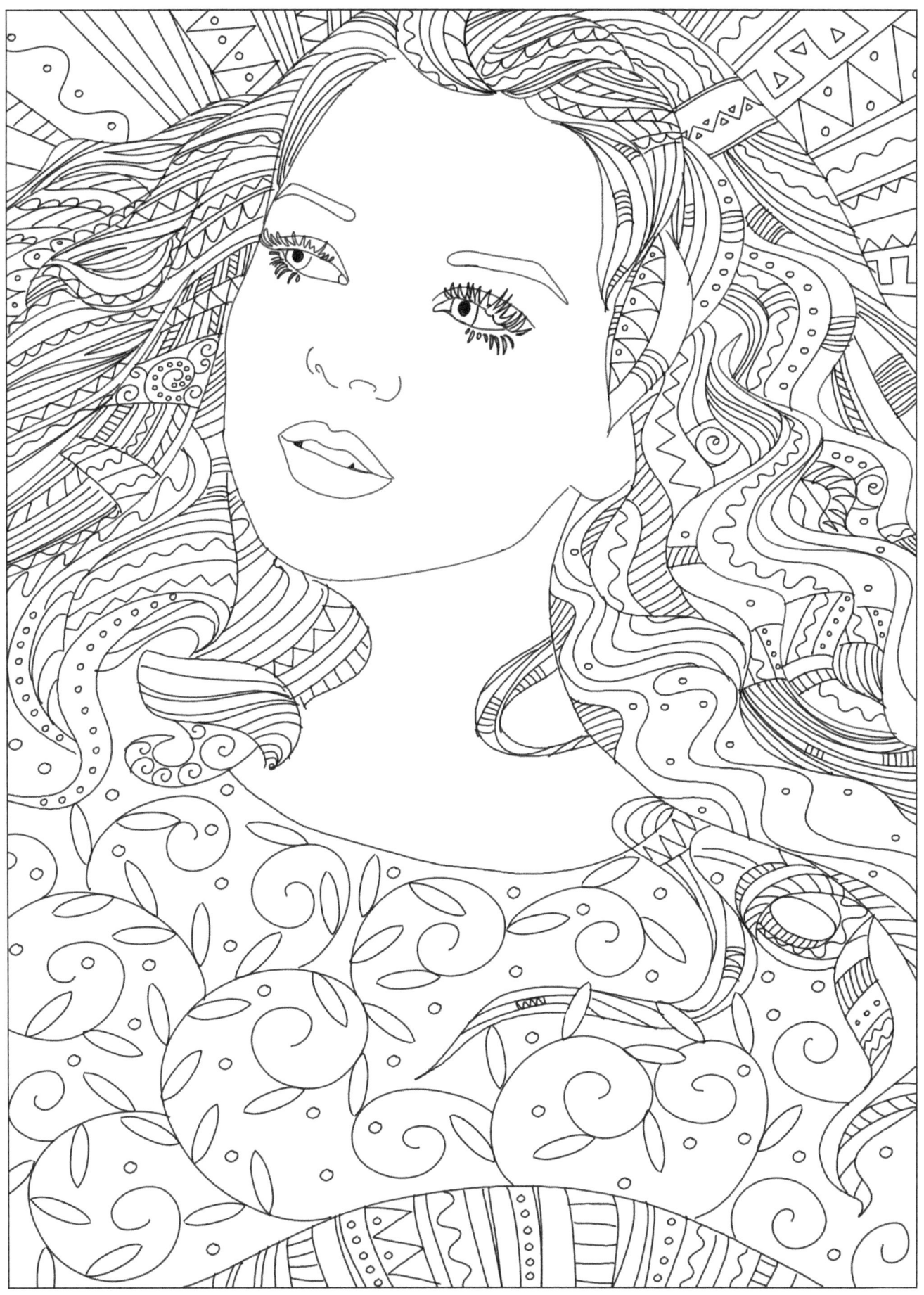

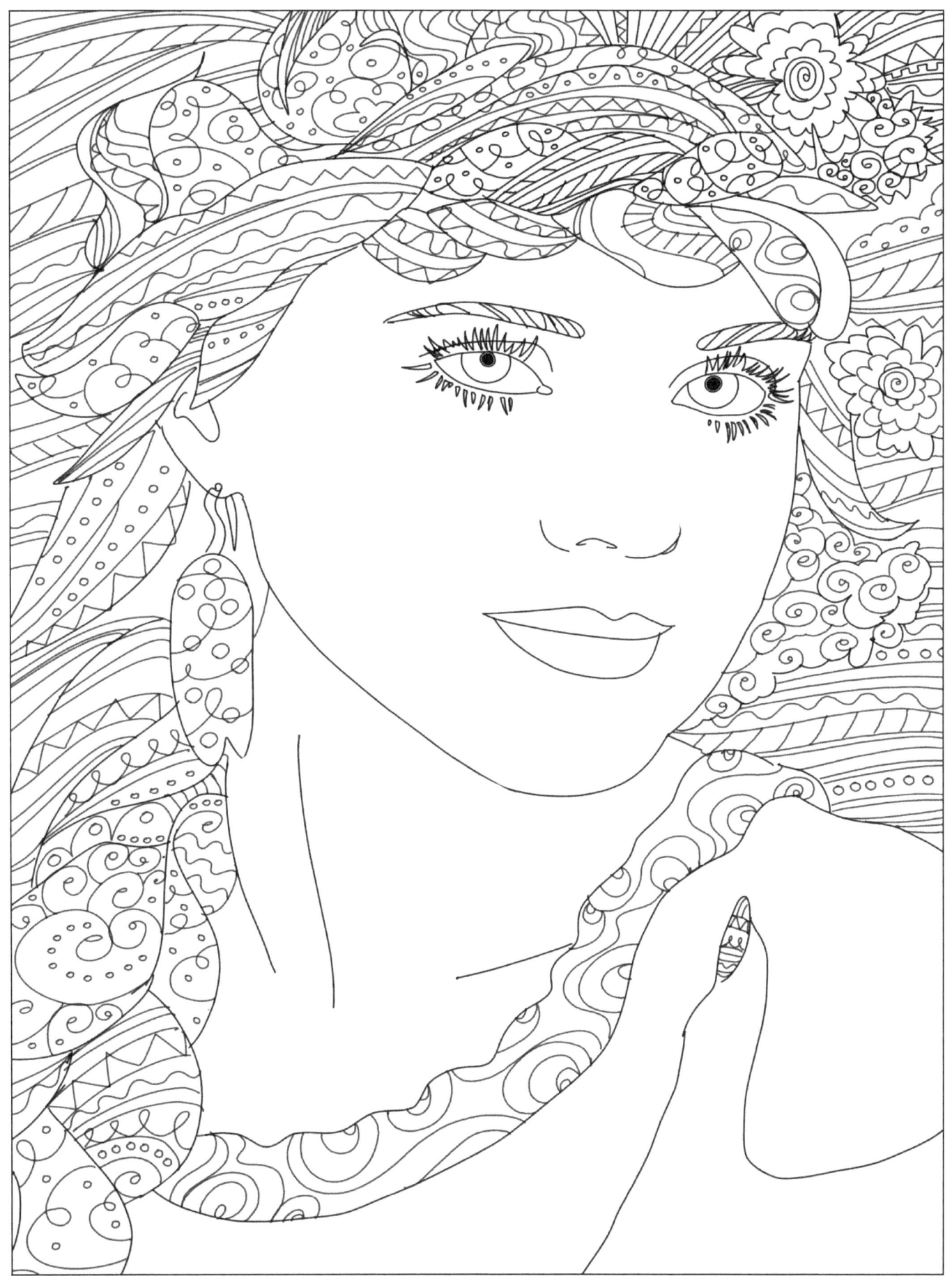

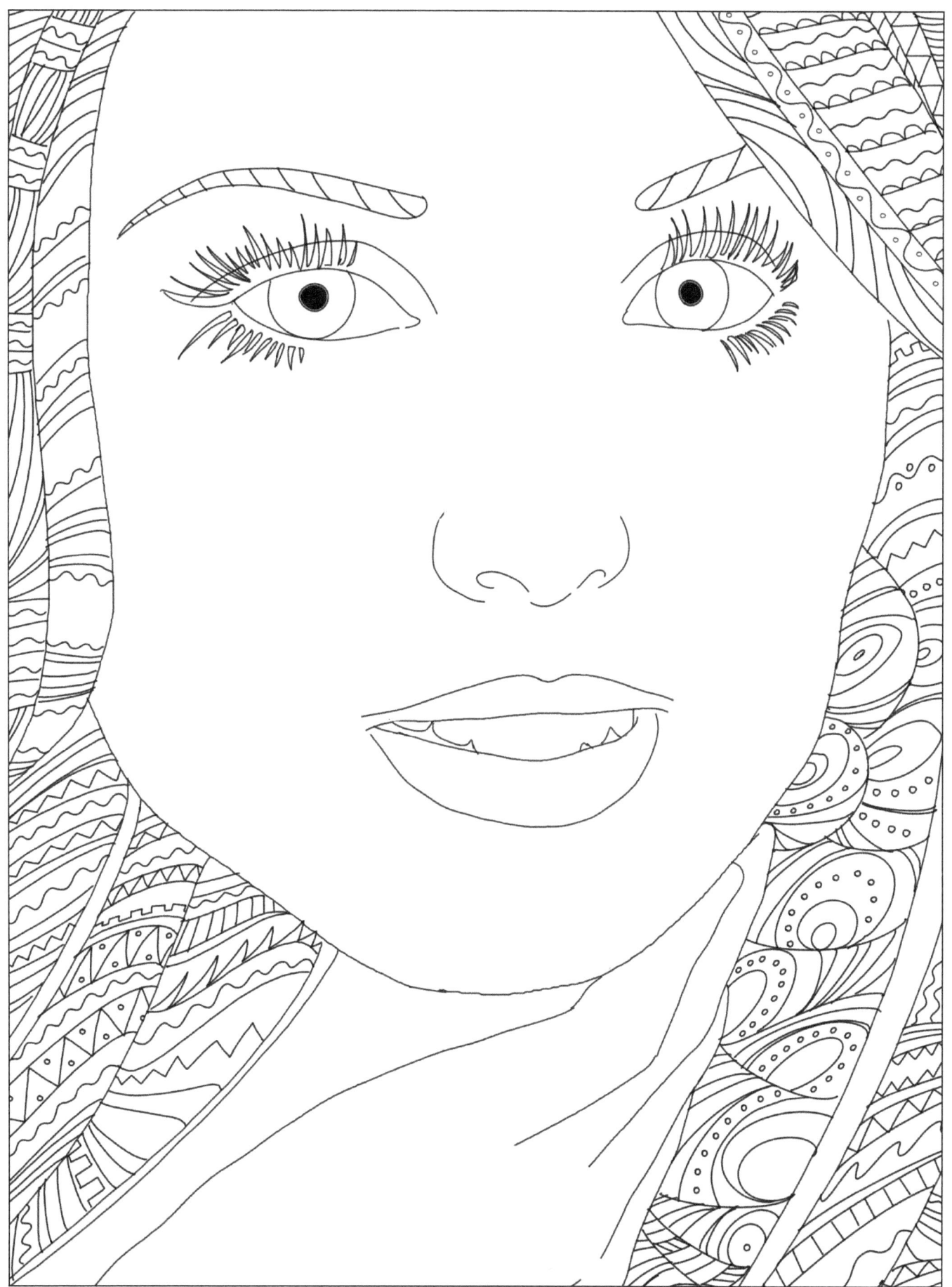

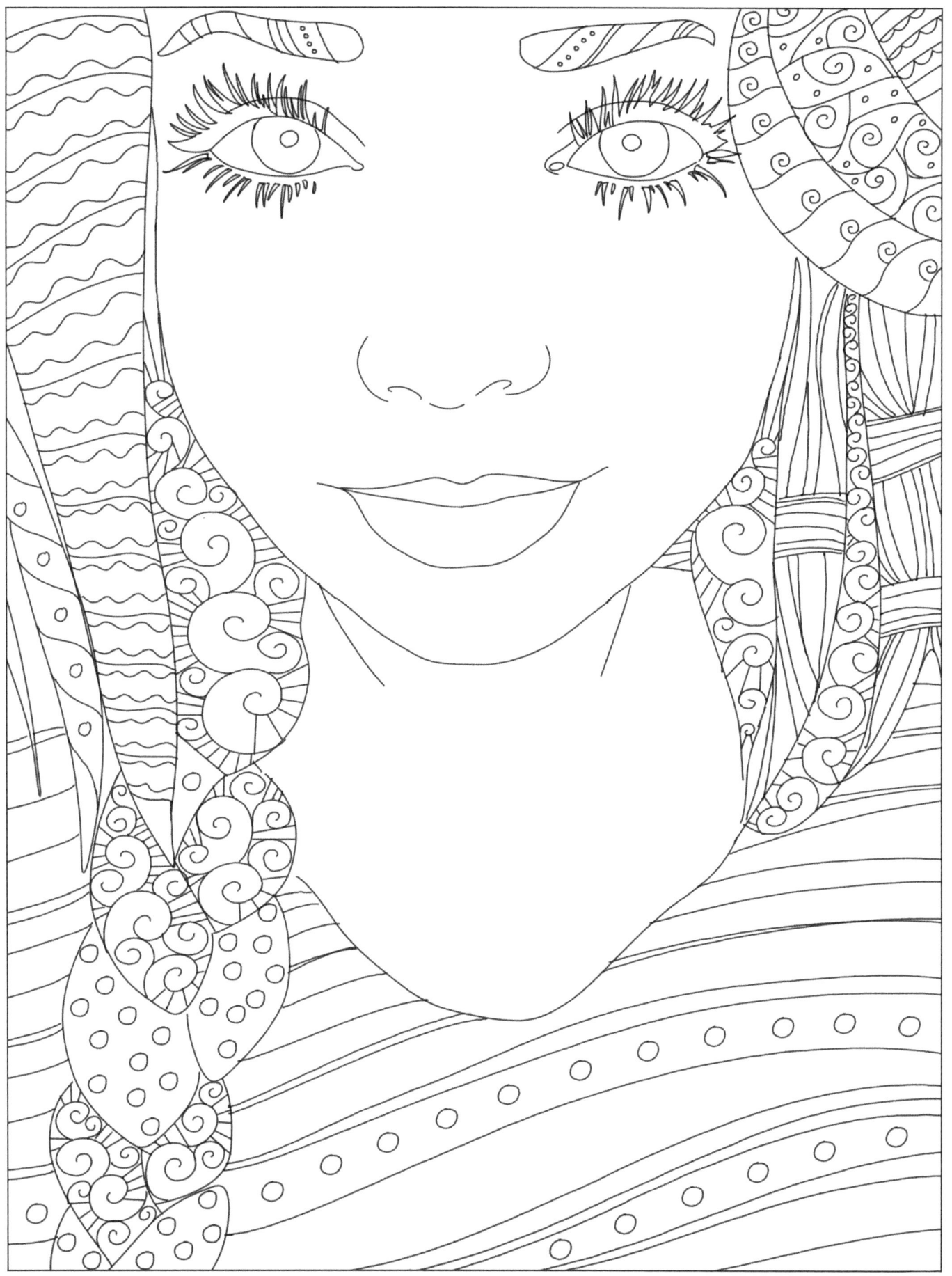

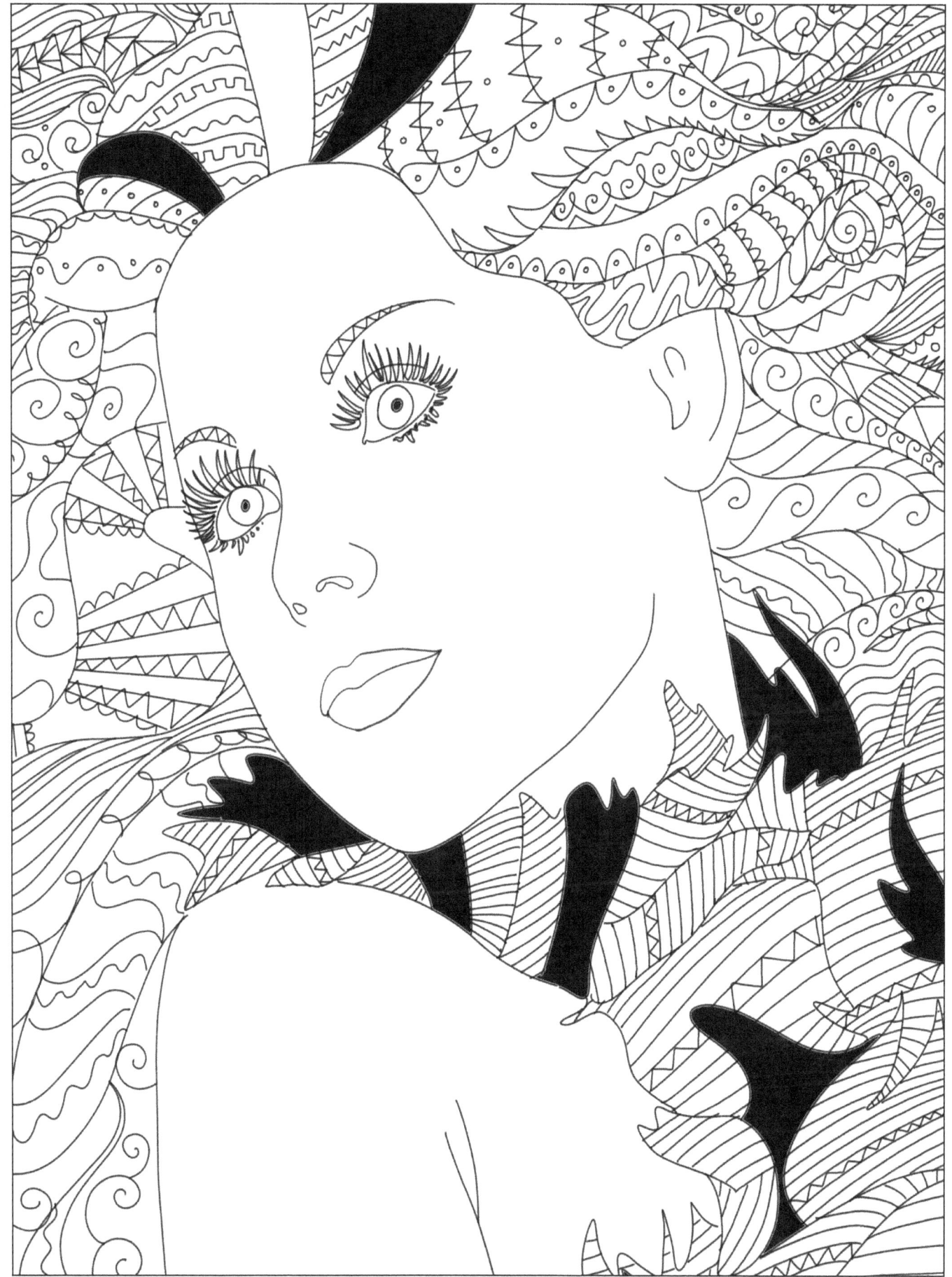

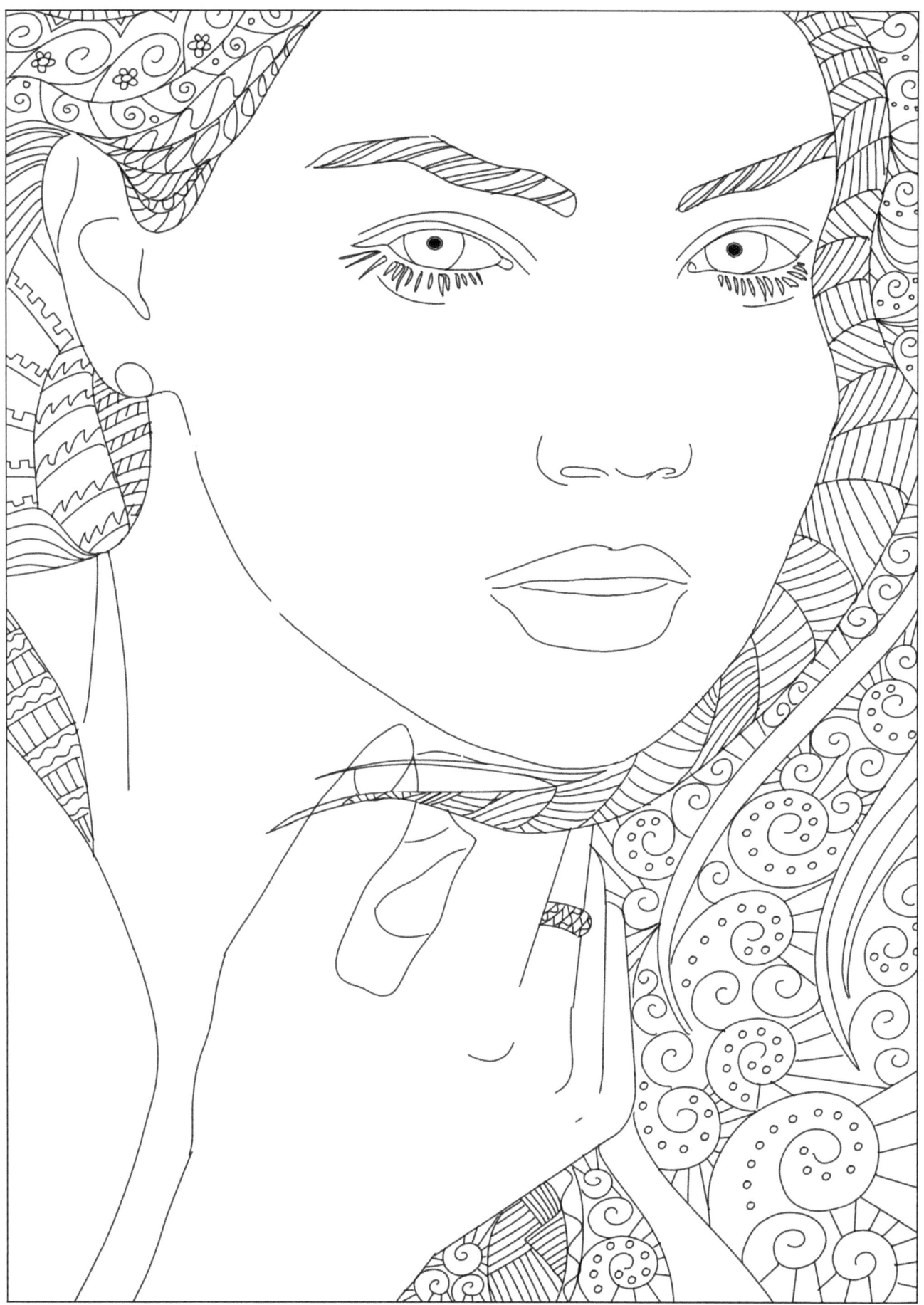

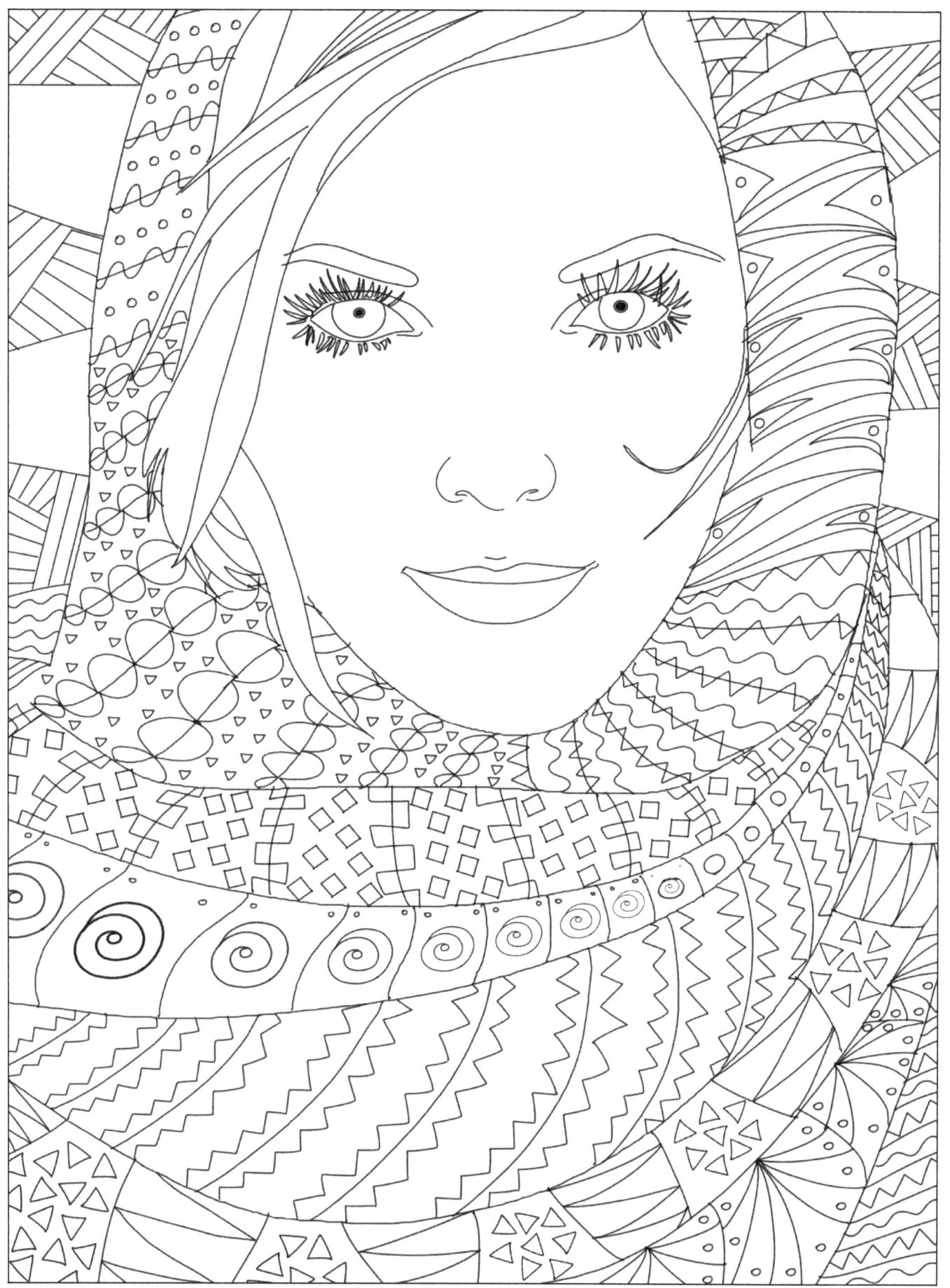

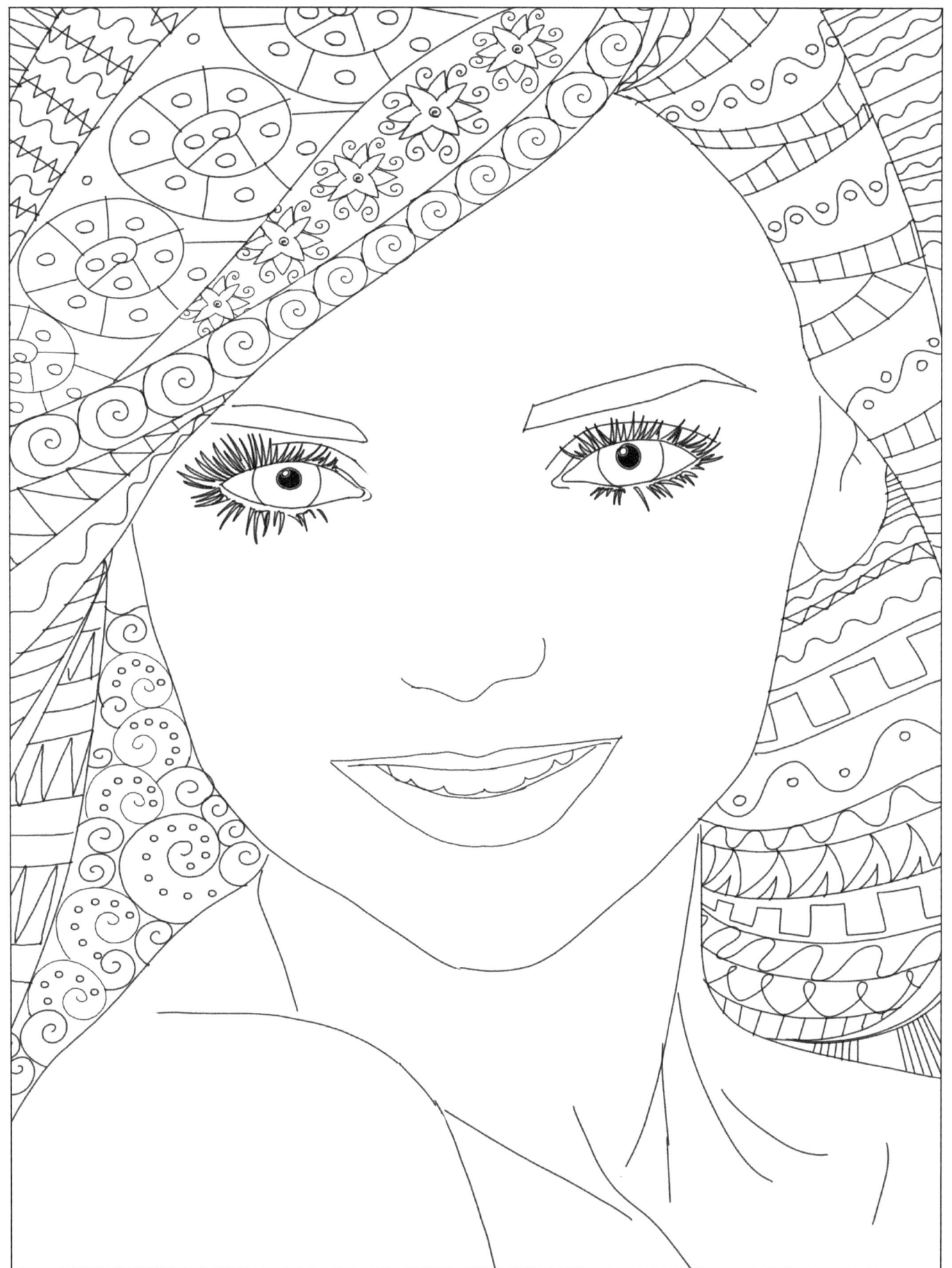

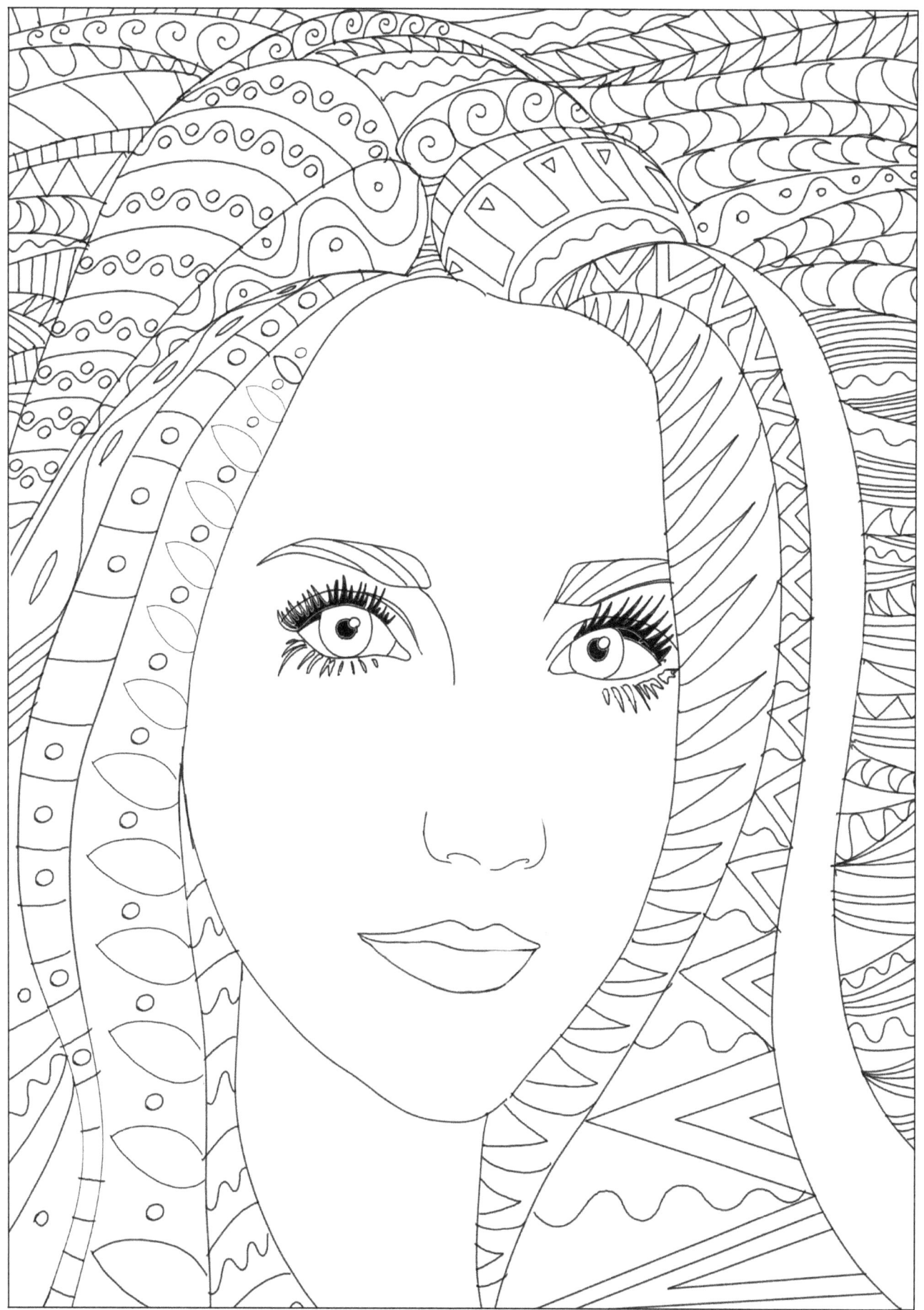

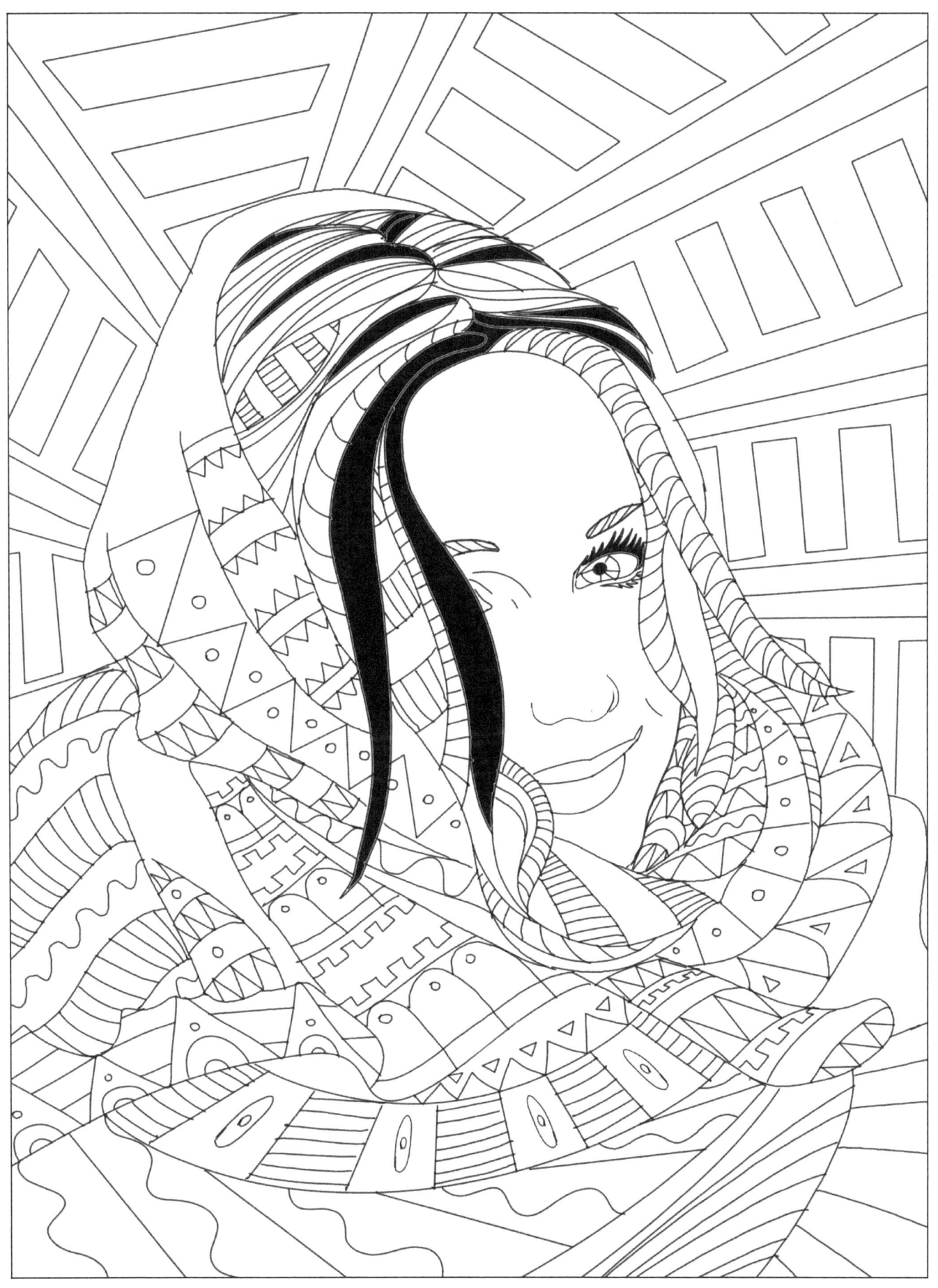

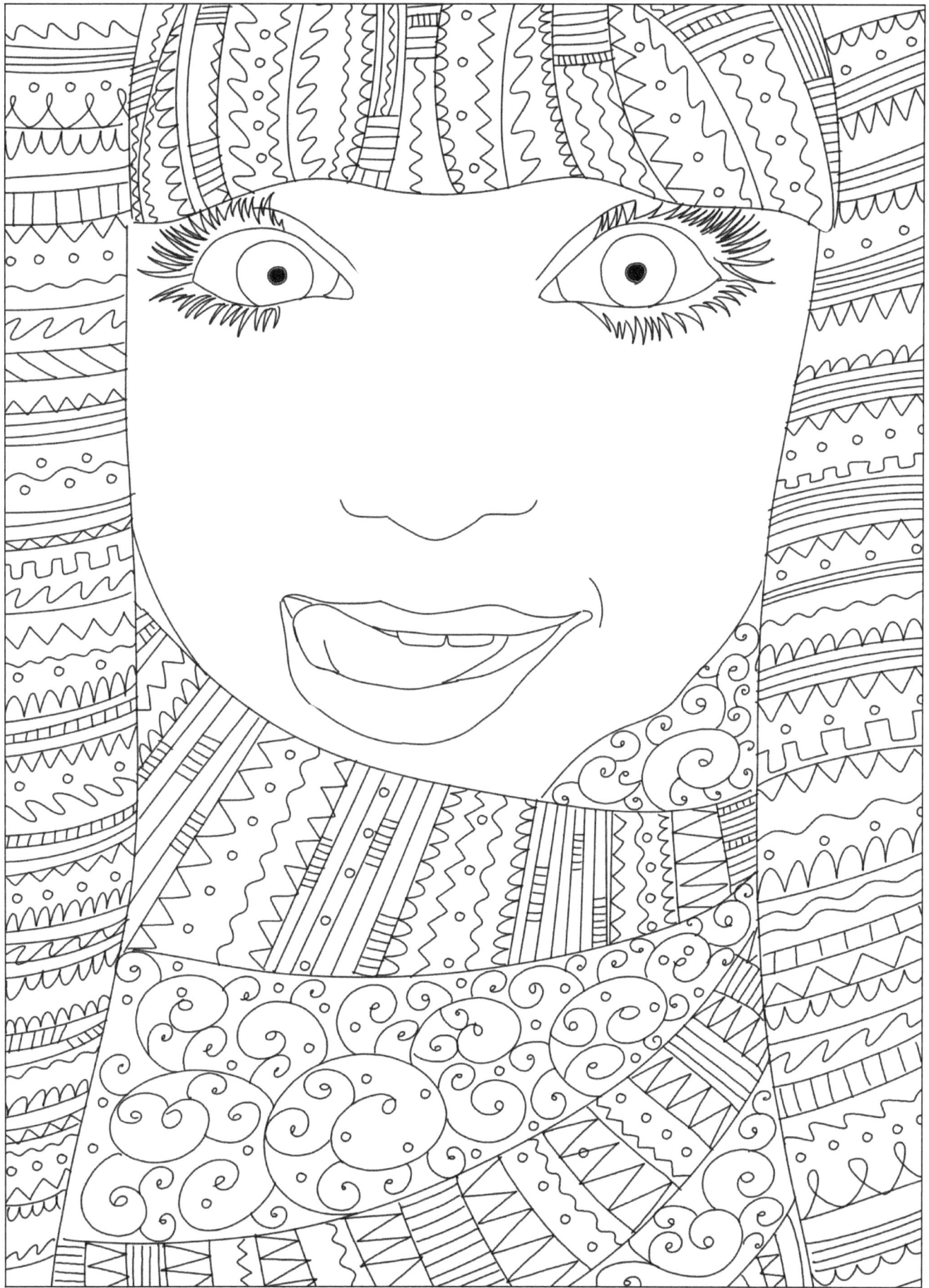

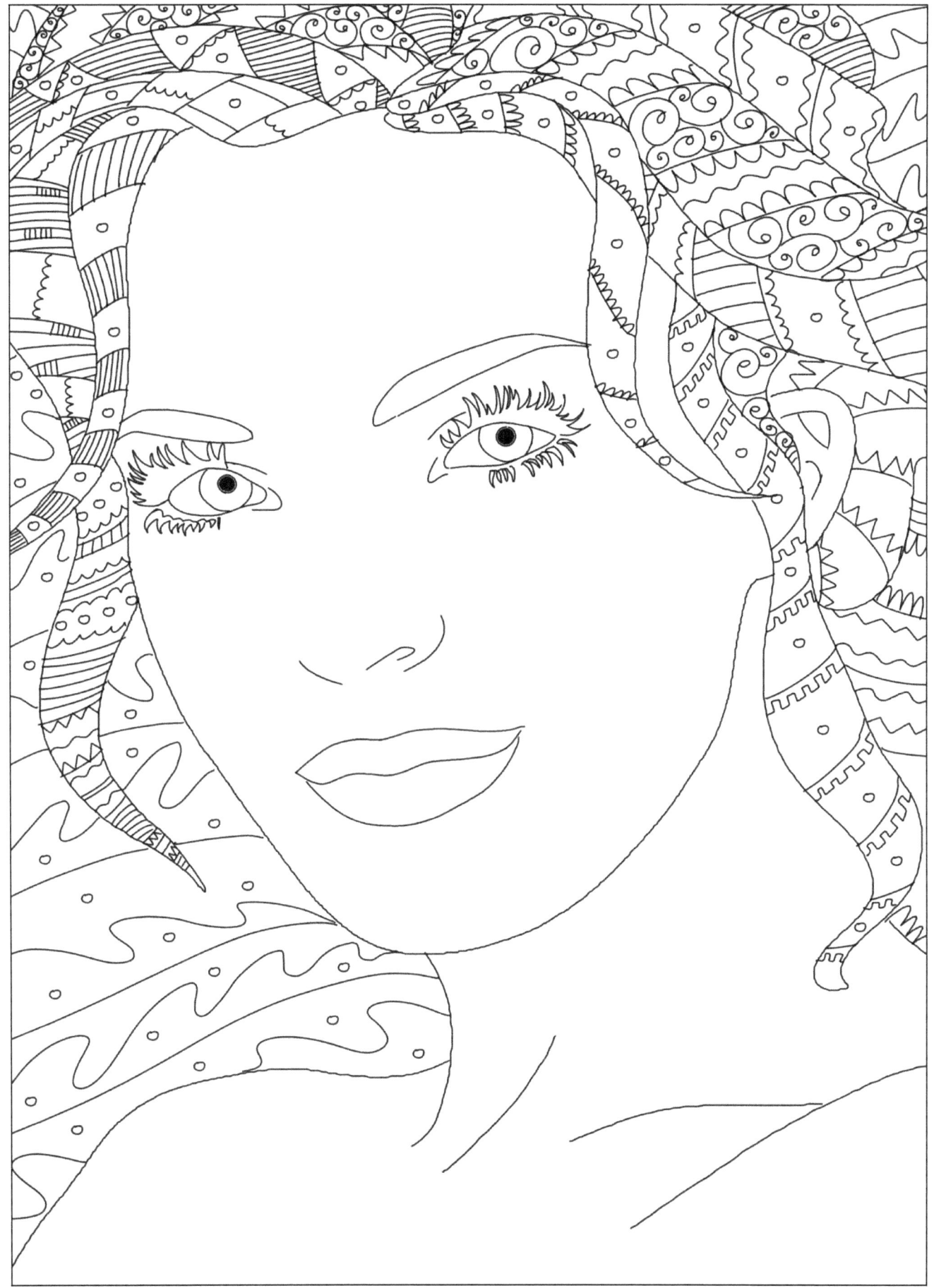

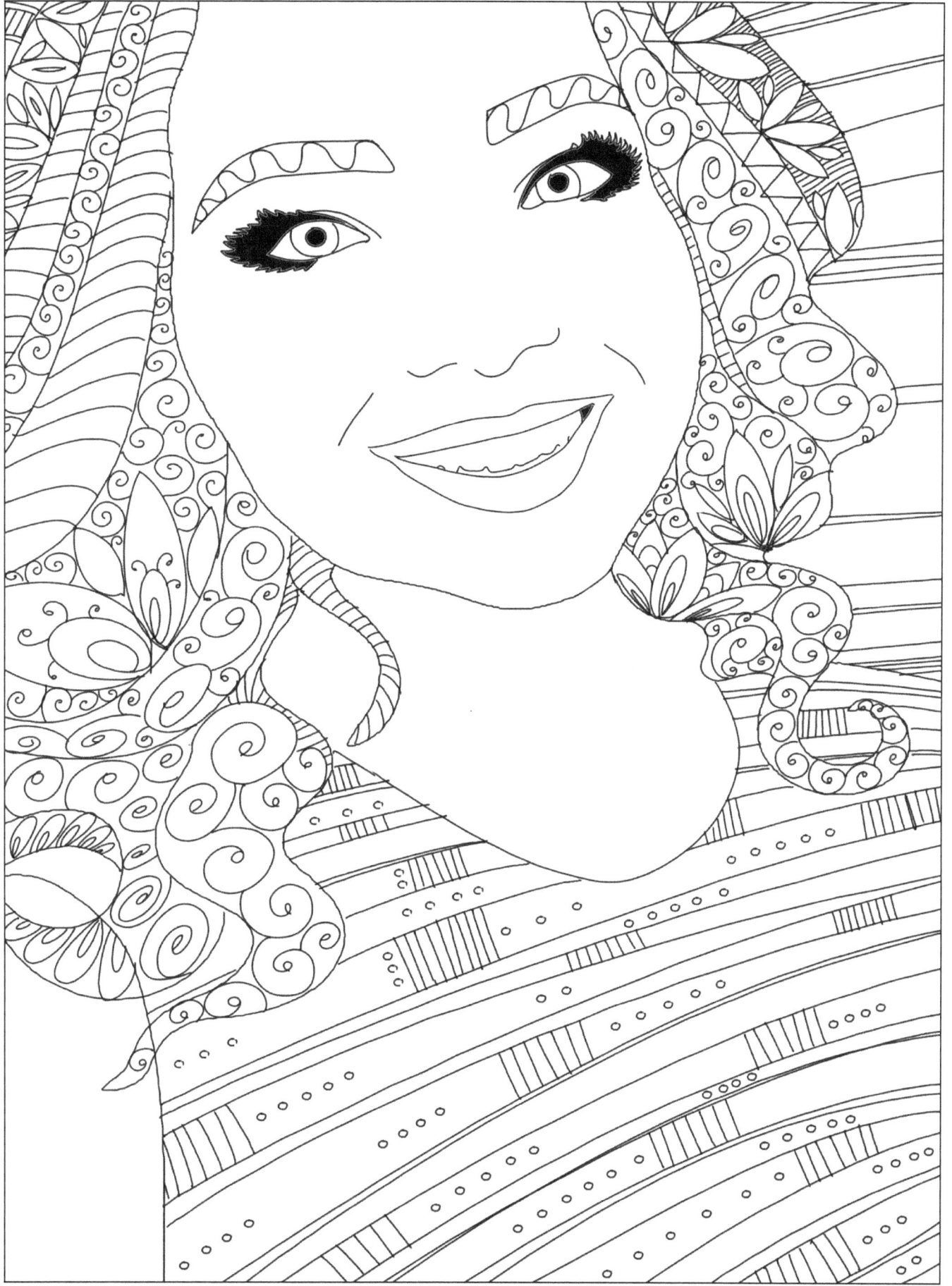

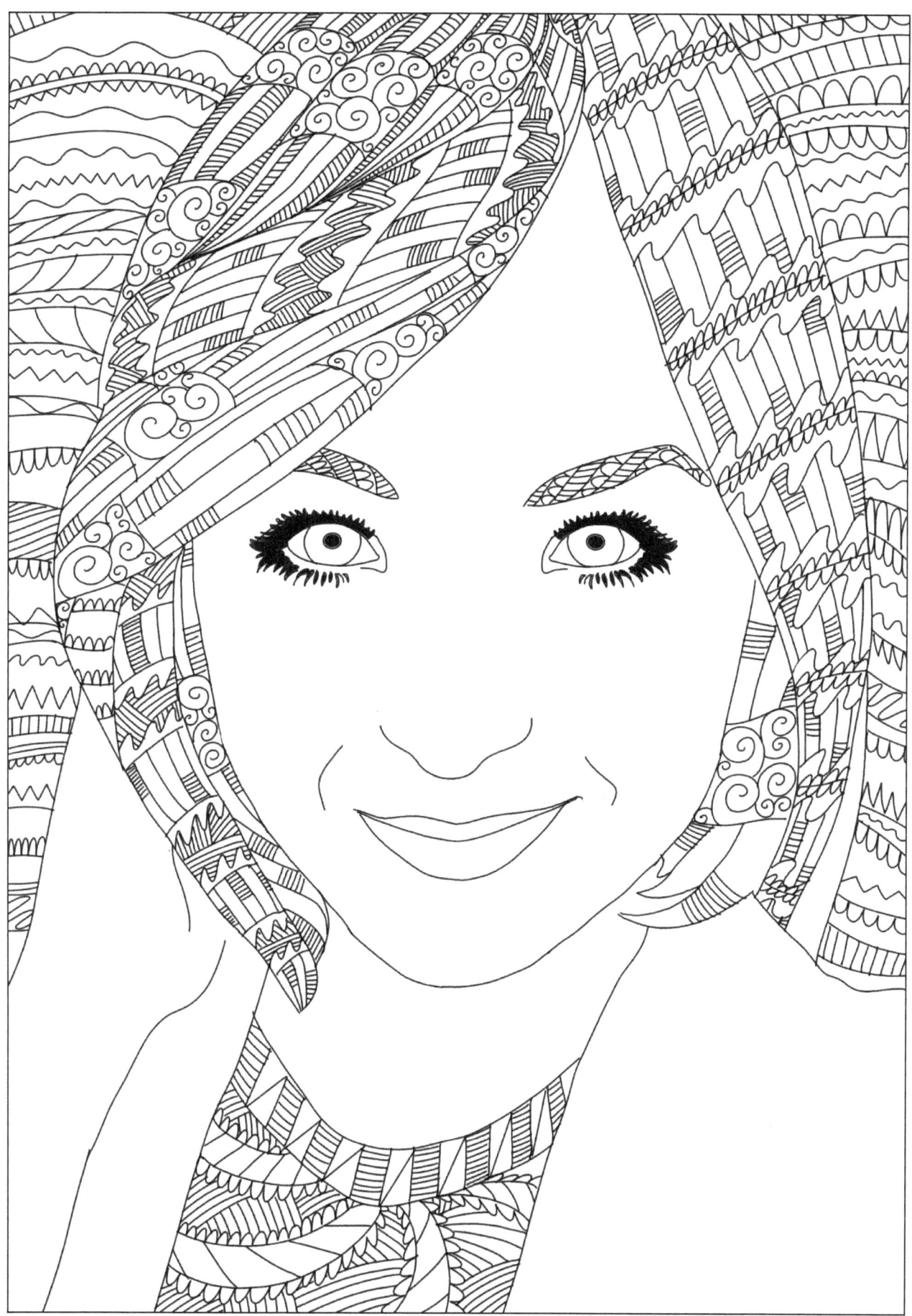

Thank you!

Thank you for choosing our book, we hope you found it interesting and helpful. If you liked the book, please give us a favor to write your review. We would really appreciate this!

If you would like to have a bonus – **FREE COLORING PAGES**, please send the screenshot of your review to this e-mail: **gloria.kemer@gmail.com** and we will send you a **FREE COLORING PAGES** in PDF as a **GIFT!****